KT-394-239

CONTENTS

ANIMALS BEHAVING BADLY

For the pupils and staff of Orchard, Southwold and
Hoxton Gardens primary schools in Hackney, who never EVER
behave badly. With thanks for your years of welcome.

First published 2017 by Walker Books Ltd
87 Vauxhall Walk, London SE11 5HJ

2 4 6 8 10 9 7 5 3 1

Text © 2017 Nicola Davies
Illustrations © 2017 Adam Stower

The right of Nicola Davies and Adam Stower to be identified as author
and illustrator respectively of this work has been asserted by them in
accordance with the Copyright, Designs and Patents Act 1988

This book has been typeset in Avenir
Printed and bound in Great Britain by Clays Ltd, St Ives plc

British Library Cataloguing in Publication Data:
a catalogue record for this book is available from the British Library

ISBN 978-1-4063-6605-1

www.walker.co.uk

ANIMALS BEHAVING BADLY

Nicola Davies

with illustrations by
Adam Stower

WALKER
BOOKS

Introduction

ANIMALS are clever. They may not drive cars or operate computers, build skyscrapers or make videos on YouTube, but they are clever in the ways they have adapted to survive in every kind of habitat, all over our planet. We need submarines to explore the sea's depths, but a sperm whale can dive to the bottom of the ocean as easily as we'd run down a flight of stairs. Without water we would die within days in the middle of a hot desert, but a kangaroo rat can live all its life without drinking. We would need a powerful saw to open the seedpods of the Brazil nut tree, but an agouti's teeth can do it in moments. The agouti's strong teeth, the sperm whale's deep diving and the kangaroo rat's ability to live without drinking are all adaptations – ways in which these animals' bodies and behaviours help them to survive in a particular habitat. But adaptations like these don't happen overnight. It takes a lot of time, thousands or even millions of years of evolution, for animals to become so well adapted to their environment and way of life.

Sadly, we humans are changing the planet around us so fast that there isn't time for animals to adapt to the changes *we* make to the places where *they* live. All over the world, all sorts of different kinds of animals are disappearing because of what humans are doing – cutting down forests, polluting rivers and seas, even changing the climate!

I don't know about you, but this makes me very sad and very cross. So I'm always happy to hear about animals that *can* get the better of humans, and manage to survive in spite of all we do to make their lives difficult and dangerous. This book is about some of those creatures. Humans say these animals are behaving badly – and a lot of other nasty things besides – because they get in our way. But the truth is, they are just surviving and being clever at it. The only really badly behaved animals on Earth are *us*.

Demon Wolverines

Y ou might not know what a wolverine is, so let me introduce you. Imagine a low-slung, weaselly sort of a beast, about the size of a Labrador dog. OK so far? Now, make its legs a bit longer and its fur thicker and shaggier.

There – you've got a wolverine!

thick dark, oily fur

big muscles

potent anal glands

strong teeth

large, five-toed paws

short legs

If a beefier, furrier kind of weasel doesn't look particularly impressive to you, then prepare to be surprised...

Near Point Hope in Alaska, in the early spring of 1944, an Inuit hunter was out on the sea ice when he saw a big male polar bear. The human and the bear were searching for the same thing – seals – but the bear found a wolverine instead. The bear, like you perhaps, was not impressed. How much trouble could an animal a fraction of its size cause? It snarled and took a lazy lunge at the big weasel.

The bear clearly didn't know much about wolverines. But it soon learnt. Instead of running off, the wolverine leapt at the bear, clamped its jaws around its windpipe, and held on until the bear was dead. An animal weighing less than a six-year-old child had just taken out the biggest land-living carnivore on Earth.

This was a surprise for the polar bear, but not for the Inuit, because although wolverines don't usually hunt on the sea ice, they have a reputation that every hunter in the far north knows.

Wolverines live from Alaska to Greenland, from Norway to the Chukchi Peninsula in Siberia: wherever the winters are long and cruel, and snow lies deep on the ground from autumn to spring. They are known to be solitary, fierce and fearless; there are reports of lone wolverines seeing off a grizzly bear or a pack of wolves. They are known to have the strength of a much larger animal; a wolverine can drag a deer carcass halfway up a mountain. And they are known for something else, too: their ability to get the better of human beings.

They are said to be "spiteful" and "devilish"; they will destroy traps and wreck human homes and food stores. "Fiend", "demon", "devil" and

"vandal" are just some of the not very com-
plimentary words that people have used to
describe wolverines.

I first got interested in wolverines when I was
a little kid, because I read another true story
called "Arch Criminal of the Wild". It went like
this. In the north of Canada, around Hudson Bay,
a Cree hunter was making his living by trapping
animals like foxes, beavers, pine martens and
wolverines, and selling their fur. Many people
did that back then and a few still do today. A
wolverine moved into the trapper's area, ripped
apart every single one of the many steel traps
he had set to catch animals, and killed his dog.
One night, while he was sleeping, it got into his
cabin and chewed through his store of furs. It
gobbled up his food and what it didn't eat, it
left ruined by the horrible stink of its musky
scent glands. It dragged his gun off into the

woods and, finally, shredded his snowshoes, which made it very difficult for him to struggle back through the snow to town and replace all he'd lost.

You could easily see this as a tall story, made up as an excuse for human mistakes – a lost gun, some broken traps – but stories like this were common. So common that a company that bought furs from hunters across Canada had a handbook for all trappers that said:

"When a wolverine moves into his territory, a trapper has but two alternatives: he must trap the wolverine or give up trapping."

The trappers of course thought wolverine trap-wrecking and food-spoiling was "wicked", but even as a little kid I was on the side of the wolverines. It seemed to me quite fair to destroy the traps, weapons and food stores of someone who was out to kill you and your kind. I especially loved the part of that story where the snow-shoes get wrecked and the gun disappears. But did the wolverine really know what it was doing?

Probably not. Wolverines survive by being able to eat anything, alive or dead. They'll catch small mammals, eat eggs, gobble up any dead body they come across. They'll chew on old skin and their jaws are so strong that they can crunch their way through bones and eat the bits just as you would eat a bag of crisps. As they can never be sure where their next meal is coming from, they can eat *a lot.* Their scientific name, *Gulo gulo*, means "glutton" twice over! They're territorial, too – they don't want to share the food on their patch. Like many mammals, their way of saying "this is mine" is to scent-mark it by squeezing the stinky, oily contents of their glands (which are like little pockets round their bottoms), all over the food.

Another way to see that wolverine's "devilish" raid on the Cree trapper is this: the wolverine found dead animals – in other words, ready-meals – in the traps. So, when it broke the traps it was simply taking the wrapper off its dinner. The food in the store was just another easy meal, and scent-marking it a way of saying "this is my nosh now". Perhaps, with the smell of human all round, the wolverine was also anxious, which would have made the scent-marking extra stinky. What about chomping the snowshoes and carrying off the gun? Well, back then snowshoes were strung with deerskin – more wolverine snacks. And the gun perhaps looked like some weird kind of bone that the wolverine could bury in the woods to eat later. As for the poor old dog, he probably just looked at Mr Wolverine the wrong way.

Seen like this, it isn't the behaviour of a

demon, taking revenge on an enemy, but that of a hungry animal trying to make the most of an opportunity. Wolverines aren't wicked or spiteful. They're just getting on with surviving in a tough environment. However, their extraordinary ability to survive gives one group of humans a very hard time indeed, and that's the scientists who study them.

Jeff Copeland, a wildlife biologist who has spent much of his life trying to find out about wolverines, described researching them as like "shadowing a ghost". Wolverines are always moving to find food; their strategy seems to be: "if you cover enough ground you're sure to find something to eat eventually". A wolverine's territory can be huge – more than twice the size of the Isle of Wight, five times bigger than Staten Island, and they can cover 30 kilometres in a day and be 800 kilometres away in a month. Mountains mean nothing to them; they can climb sheer cliffs and disappear into the next valley in hours. Wolverines can cope with this constant marathon because they have extra big hearts and lungs. Their bodies burn up food to produce energy faster than other animals of the same size. Huge feet spread their weight, so they can run over snow without sinking in, and their long claws act like the metal spikes that hikers and climbers have on their boots, so they can scramble up ice-covered slopes.

All this makes wolverines extremely difficult to follow. No human can keep up with them on foot and of course they don't live in places where there are many roads. So for years, pretty much all that people knew about them was their reputation: *the demon vandal that walks alone*. The invention of electronic tracking devices small enough to be attached to animals' bodies and powerful enough to beam signals over several kilometres, gave scientists a chance to find out more for the first time.

But to use a tracking device, you first have to catch a wolverine.

A wolverine trap needs to be strong. When you're making one, your first move is to cut down some trees. Big trees. Then you chop them up and make a sort of mini log cabin. The logs that form the walls must be joined together tightly, with no gaps, or the wolverine will chew its way out. The log lid must be heavy to keep the demon beast inside. Mark Scafford is studying wolverines in Alberta, Canada – and when I asked him, "How heavy?" he told me, "Oh, about one hundred pounds. Maybe more? One hundred and twenty?" That's a weight of 100 pounds to keep an animal that weighs less than 40 pounds inside.

To set the trap, you lift the lid (feeling strong?). It will fall when the wolverine pulls on the bait, a juicy bit of dead beaver attached to a strong steel wire at the back of the trap. When that happens, the gadget you've attached to the lid will send a *bleep* to your phone, telling you the trap is sprung.

Now, all you need to do is to get a wild wolverine to go inside. Hopefully you've built your trap somewhere where there are likely to be wolverines – out on a mountain where you've already seen their tracks. But your trap is just one place in a wolverine territory that could stretch out for kilometres in every direction. How will they find it? Smell! The smelliest smell you can make. Mix up some skunk extract (yes, there really is something called "skunk extract", a liquid that smells like skunks), beaver oil and rancid fish oil, put it in a container and string it high in a tree where the wind can spread that *delicious* pong on the breeze. With luck, the fine-tuned wolverine nose will pick it up from far away.

But the sense of smell that brings the wolverine to the trap will also pick up your scent

on it. Any wolverine that turns up will be very, very wary.

Let's face it, your chances of success are pretty slim. You're going to have to make and set a lot of traps. You have long days and nights of work ahead of you, in freezing conditions. Oh and, I forgot to say: all of this has to be done in midwinter, when the bears are asleep, or they'll just steal your bait and wreck your traps. At this time of year, temperatures in wolverine habitats go down to minus 30 °C, and lower. Inside its fur coat, the wolverine will be toasty; inside your layers of clothing, you may freeze. You are going to have to become "a person with no quit in them", as folk say in wolverine country.

If you get really lucky, the lure of a free meal may be too much for a hungry wolverine to resist. A *bleep* sounds on your phone, telling you the trap is sprung! From that moment the clock is ticking. You have to get to that trap before the wolverine finds its way out. No matter what time of day or night, no matter how bad the conditions, you have to get there, even if it means skiing through a blizzard for two hours in the middle of the night. When you arrive at the trap, you'll hear a deep, angry growling that will make your hair stand on end. This is the creature that sees off bears, remember. It survives by being able to stand up to *anything*. It is an animal "with no quit in it". And it's in your trap. How on Earth are you going to get it out and put a radio tag on it?

Very, very carefully you lift the lid of the trap (still feeling strong?). The wolverine may jam its snout through the gap, revealing an impressive set of teeth. That's when you jab it with an anaesthetic syringe, attached to the end of a long stick. You drop the lid and wait. Some wolverines are so tough they need more than one dose to put them to sleep.

Once you're *sure* it's asleep, you lift it out very carefully and attach the collar with the radio-tracking device inside. It will track the wolverine's position for as long as the battery lasts. You put the sleepy demon back in the trap to recover safely.

Later, at dawn perhaps, as you watch the wolverine climb out of the trap (probably carrying the beaver bait if it hasn't eaten it all already), you cross your fingers and hope that it doesn't just rip the collar off and chew it to bits. And all that effort is just the start, because to really find out what wolverines get up to, you need to put tracking devices on more than just one!

In spite of all the things about wolverines that make them very hard to study, some tough, determined field biologists have stuck with it, and, over the last two decades, learnt a lot about them. It turns out their reputation for being lonesome has no truth in it. Males and females hang out together sometimes, and their children – called kits – spend time with mum and dad after they grow up. Wolverines even play.

However their reputation for amazing toughness is supported by what the scientists have discovered. The tracking device from one male wolverine revealed that it had climbed a 3,190-metre mountain, going up the sheer rock face in a midwinter blizzard. It covered the last and steepest stretch in an hour and a half. Human climbers tried to repeat this feat the following summer, and just gave up. It was too hard.

As always, no matter how much trouble animals give us, we always give them more. Ever-wandering wolverines need a lot of space, and we humans are filling that wild space with towns and roads, mines and factories. Wolverines need a cold climate and we are making the places where they live ever warmer. So, I'm glad to hear stories about the wildness and mischief of wolverines.

Here's something one wildlife cameraman, John Aitchison, told me. Not long ago, an American Indian hunter called George Wholecheese came upon a wolverine along a frozen riverbed in Alaska. Wolverine fur is highly prized for being frost-resistant, so when George's snowmobile got stuck in a drift he was disappointed. There wasn't time to reach for his rifle, so he threw an axe at the animal. It missed and landed in the snow.

The wolverine sauntered over, peed on the axe and walked off.

As the wolverine biologist Doug Chadwick wrote, "There's wild, and then there's wolverine!"

Kea Crime

E VERY year, thousands of tourists come to the beautiful mountains of New Zealand's South Island to see the places where the *Lord of the Rings* and *Hobbit* movies were filmed. Of course there are no real Nazgûl or dragons swooping down from the sky, but there is a different kind of winged menace. It's called a kea, and it's one of New Zealand's native parrots. (You can use the same word, kea, for one kea or lots of them – you don't need an "s" on the end.)

clever brain

yellow nostrils

sharp blue beak

red flash under the wing

dull green feathers

nimble feet

Kea don't look like anything special. They're about the size of a crow, and they don't have pretty feathers, just a sort of dull green (though they do have a nifty flash of scarlet under their wings). But if you park your car or pitch your tent in kea country, you might find out the hard way what makes them remarkable. While you're out pretending to be Bilbo or Aragorn striding across the mountain landscape, the kea may pay you a visit. They'll snip the guy ropes of your tent, shred your sleeping bag and then carry off your cooking gear. They'll pull the rubber from your windscreen wipers and from round your car windows; they'll bend the aerial. If they have enough time, they'll peck out the lights and chomp through any loose cables they find. If they get inside the car, by the time you get back, its seats will look as if they've exploded, ripped to shreds with the stuffing pulled out.

This kind of vandalism takes time: a few hours perhaps. But you only have to turn your back for a moment for kea to get up to *something*. One visitor, Peter Marshall from Glasgow, had all his holiday money snatched from his car when a kea leaned in through an open window. Another Scottish visitor lost his passport to a thieving kea. In winter, skiers are forever having their gloves snatched – kea just adore pulling the stuffing out of thermal mitts!

Even when a kea is safely behind bars it can go on giving humans the runaround. In San Diego Zoo, a kea called Lucy learnt how to break the lock on her cage – and on all the other birds' cages. Wayne Schulberg, the animal-care manager, arrived one morning to find all the aviaries empty and all the birds flying free.

It's hard to see what a parrot would do with a thousand dollars and a passport, but some kea crimes are easier to understand. Stealing food is their speciality. Kea will fly down chimneys to raid the pantry of a ski lodge while people are out on the slopes. They'll knock over rubbish bins to sort through what's inside and pick out anything yummy. If you leave a window even a tiny bit open they will sample every single thing in your kitchen.

Kea are especially fond of butter and fat, and this has got them into real trouble over the years. Back in the 1860s, kea started to land on the backs of sheep, digging through their wool and skin to get to the fat underneath. Scientists think they may have learnt to do this by picking the maggots out of dead sheep, discovering by accident that live sheep were tasty too. However the kea came to do it, sheep attacked in this way often died from blood loss or when their wounds became infected. New Zealand farmers were *furious* and for a hundred years kea had a bounty on their heads. More than 150,000 birds were poisoned and shot, and to this day there is a type of shotgun known as a "kea gun".

Hunting kea is now banned, and they are protected by the New Zealand government. But they still sometimes make holes in sheep and eat their fat, and they regularly wreck cars and damage houses and campsites. Anything that isn't locked up or tied down might be attacked by kea. People who live on South Island know all doors must be locked and all windows shuttered whenever they go out, and that every loose wire or cable must be protected from getting "kea-ed". Mostly South Islanders are used to this, but once in a while someone loses patience and takes a shot at the feathery vandals.

What makes kea behave this way when most of their raids seem to be about creating mayhem rather than getting food? Scientists Judy Diamond and Alan Bond have studied kea for years, and once watched a young male roll up a heavy rubber mat, perhaps twice his own weight, then push it off the porch where the home-owner had spread it. Why? "A lot of the time, what kea do is to get human attention," Judy says. "They know that human attention means, somewhere along the line, they'll get fed."

There are signs everywhere in kea country telling people not to feed them, but tourists find their mischief irresistible – especially when it's someone else's car that gets trashed, not theirs. Kea often get rewarded for naughtiness, so they learn that someone will pay them for their tricks.

"Kea are controlling what we do!" Alan told me with a big grin.

That's just part of the story. Another reason for their endless mischief is that kea love anything new. Most birds are wary of new objects in their environment, but kea go straight up and investigate, prodding and probing, pulling and twisting, holding and throwing. They seem to be thinking: *poke it, bite it, tweak it, see what it does.* They can do almost anything with any object because their beaks are especially adaptable – narrower and longer than most other parrots. So adaptable, in fact, that the kea beak is sometimes described as a bird Swiss army knife, after the penknife with lots of pull-out attachments from scissors to screwdrivers.

Their ability to adapt, plus their curiosity, helped kea to survive in their tough mountain habitat before humans came along. Back then, kea were quite rare. They were surrounded by many other kinds of native New Zealand birds. Each species was really good at eating one type of food in one kind of way. These super-efficient specialist birds left very little food for the poor old kea. So they had to learn to be adaptable – to eat whatever was left over, whatever they could get, wherever and whenever they could get it. They grubbed up beetles and worms from the soil with their beaks, they ate berries, nectar and seeds, they even went down seabird nest-burrows to pull out the fat chicks and make a meal of them.

Then Europeans came along and everything changed. They didn't live alongside nature as the native people, the Māori, had always done. Instead, they cut down forests to make grasslands for the sheep they brought with them and accidentally let loose rats and cats, which had never lived in New Zealand before. Many of the specialist birds died out, killed either by the introduced animals or because of the destruction of their forest home and the loss of the special foods it had provided. But kea didn't depend on just one sort of food – they could *already* eat *anything*. So when sheep died on the hillside or when a farmer threw out the remains after a lamb that had been killed for dinner, the kea feasted. Pretty soon they weren't rare any more, and soon after that, a reward was offered for every dead kea.

A beak like a toolkit, huge curiosity and a history of making the most out of the opportunities that humans provide; these are three of the secrets to the kea's successful life of crime. Another is their brain: kea are perhaps the cleverest birds in the world. Intelligence tests with captive and wild kea show that they are often cleverer than crows and can even do some puzzles that monkeys or small children would struggle over. They're good at solving several problems in a row, too. One test involved seven different tasks that had to be done in order before the bird got a food reward: a kea did them all in under a minute.

And kea also learn from each other. In one test, the first kea took a few minutes of trial and error to work out how to thread two plastic rings off a stick in order to get to one of their favourite foods – butter. A second bird stood by and watched, and when it came to that bird's turn to solve the puzzle, it did it straightaway. "When kea encounter a new object," Judy explained, "they wave it around to get the attention of other kea." Investigating a new object together is part of their social life; think of how you invite your friends round to play when you have a new computer game. "All parrots are very sociable," Alan told me. "If you watch other birds sitting on a wire, they're like beads, evenly spaced out. But parrots will land in little groups cuddled up together. Being sociable is how they deal with the world!"

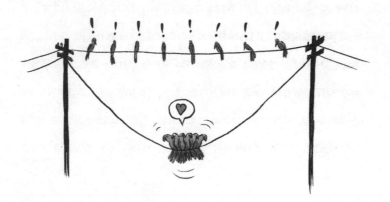

Kea do seem to like having partners in crime. Typically the worst and most damaging raids on cars are carried out by groups of kea, each taking a small part in the destruction, as if it was some kind of party. Once a group of kea start pulling something apart they will return time and time again. Judy and Alan watched some young kea utterly destroy a stuffed armchair, ripping it and pulling out the stuffing until, after a few weeks, it was just a bare wooden frame.

Perhaps the biggest reason of all behind kea crime is play. Kea, especially young kea, love to play. They play-fight, rolling over and over on the ground and wrestling like puppies. They'll hang upside down by one foot like a kid on monkey bars. They take turns knocking each other off branches. Sometimes they play on their own. A bus driver on South Island got used to a kea holding onto the windscreen of his bus as he accelerated. When the bus was going too fast for the bird to keep hold, it would let go and somersault back over the bus roof like a blown leaf. Some kea seem addicted to thrills.

All in all, kea naughtiness has helped them to adapt quickly to huge changes in their environment and to survive where other kinds of birds have been wiped out. But for all their cleverness, kea don't know everything and sometimes their pranks do them no good.

One of the many animals that have been introduced into New Zealand is the rabbit. Without the predators from the rabbits' home to keep their numbers down, they multiplied until there were rabbits everywhere. So another animal was introduced: the stoat (a bigger version of a weasel and a much smaller version of a wolverine). It was hoped that they'd gobble up the bunnies, but instead they gobbled up the native birds. Before the Europeans came along, the only mammals in New Zealand were bats. The birds had all evolved without having to think about nasty little predators like stoats, so many of them nested on the ground or in burrows – easy pickings for a hungry stoat. Kea also nest on the ground in holes and hollows in the mountain forests. The stoats and possums are eating so many kea eggs and young that the future of kea – along with other birds – could be threatened. So people who wanted to safeguard the birds began setting traps for the stoats. The trouble was, something kept triggering the traps, causing them to snap shut before they'd caught a single one. What was doing it?

A student called Mat Goodman decided to investigate. He set up video cameras near the traps, which would start filming whenever some-thing moved in front of them – and found the culprit. The creatures spoiling the stoat-catching were kea! Because they like fiddling about with any new object they come across, the kea had found out how to trigger the traps. It wasn't easy. Each trap had to be poked with a stick in exactly the right place. And not just any old stick would do. A kea had to make the right kind, by pulling off the side branches and whittling it to the right shape. Then the stick had to be pushed hard into a small slot on one end of the trap. And the kea weren't even doing this for food because the bait in the traps was untouched.

The birds of course had no idea what a big deal this was. They didn't know that by making the right sort of stick, they had joined a very special club of animals: ones that make tools. Its only members are a few kinds of birds, some monkeys, chimps and humans. The other thing they didn't know was that they were helping the stoats to keep eating their eggs and young.

The only thing the kea knew was that when one of the traps was triggered it made a great, big, gorgeous, loud *BANG!* And that was fun!

Nightmare Noises

IT'S the middle of the night. You want to be asleep SO badly, but a noise is keeping you awake. You put your fingers in your ears, wrap a pillow round your head, but nothing shuts it out.

It's a low, rhythmic *buzz, buzz, buzz*, that seems to ooze from the walls. What's causing it? Could it be the students next door, having a late party? The old central heating boiler? Or even the freezer in the basement? You don't know. All you know is that while it's in your ears, you are never going to get to sleep.

All of us have probably had an experience like that, but imagine it happening night after night after night. It's the sort of thing that drives people nuts. Scientific research has shown that low, repeating sounds have an effect on humans that you can measure: it reduces our ability to think clearly and perform simple tasks; it makes us feel sick, angry and just plain miserable.

So, it's no wonder that back in January 2005, the residents of Cape Coral in southern Florida were getting pretty fed up. A deep, droning, drumming sound was vibrating through their houses every night after dark. They knew it couldn't be the metro rumbling beneath them, or jets overhead, because Cape Coral is a quiet little city on the coast, specially built to give the people who live there as much seaside as possible. The houses are placed not only on roads, but along 600 kilometres of seawater canals (more than Venice and Amsterdam put together), so you can park your boat by your back door. The people of Cape Coral were furious that their peace and quiet was being wrecked. They were convinced that the city council was responsible; surely, they thought, the water pipes or the roads or *something* the council had done was causing the nighttime noise. Residents demanded action, and in desperation the Cape Coral council decided to employ a firm of engineers to try and get rid of the noise, at a cost of 47,000 dollars.

The work would have gone ahead and the

council would have wasted a lot of money, but luckily for them, a young biologist called James Locascio saw a headline in a local newspaper: "Noise May Cost City Big Bucks". Just hours before the city council handed over the money to the engineers, he rang them up and told them the cause of their noise nightmare. It wasn't anything to do with gurgling pipes or grumbling machinery. It was a fish.

Many people think that the undersea world is silent, but when you put a waterproof microphone – a hydrophone – over the side of a boat and listen in, you soon begin to hear crackles and clicks, clangs and moans, all manner of strange sounds, many of which may seem, to your ears, more like machines than animals.

Back in 1984, I was sailing the Indian Ocean on a small boat with some whale scientists.

As we sat on deck one evening sipping beers, we heard a deep, throbbing hum through the hydrophone. The sound was incredibly loud and exactly like an engine. We leapt up in alarm, convinced a massive container ship was about to crash into us. But there was nothing on the sea from horizon to horizon – except the blow of a whale about a hundred metres away. The sound pounding through the hydrophone was a blue whale making the deep humming sound that these creatures use to communicate over huge distances.

It's not surprising that animals in the sea use sound to talk to each other and find their way around. In deep water, there isn't enough light to see by, and even close to the surface waves, sand, mud and plankton can make the water murky. Sound travels four and a half times more quickly in water, which means that messages sent using sound travel faster and further in the sea than they can in the air. Scientists think that blue whales can hear each other across hundreds of kilometres of ocean. But it isn't only whales and dolphins that make noises in the sea – it's fish, too. They don't have vocal cords like we do, but they do have a little bag of gas in their bodies called a swim bladder, which is used to stop them sinking. They can vibrate this like the skin on a drum to make a

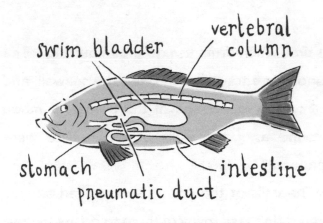

swim bladder
vertebral column
stomach
pneumatic duct
intestine

variety of different noises. Which brings us back to that young biologist...

James was studying several species of fish in the ocean off the Florida coast, and had spent hundreds of hours listening to the sounds they made in their mating season. When he read the description of the noises bothering Cape Coral householders, he was sure he knew the culprit: the black drum fish. When James visited some of the affected houses he was even more certain. "The sounds started around dusk and peaked around ten p.m.," James told me. This matched the time when drum fish do their courting. "The sounds were travelling through the seawall, and up into the foundation of the homes. It made it sound as if the walls of the houses were breathing!"

The calls of the drum fish travelled so well that it didn't take many of them to create a noise loud enough to keep people awake.

"It only takes a few fish to reach disturbance levels," James told me. "I'd estimate only tens of fish." And the houses were right on the canals, less than 100 metres away from where the fish were ... well, what were they doing exactly? Were the sounds made to call to females, or to defend territories for egg-laying? "Unfortunately," James said, "we don't have any direct observations to be able to answer this. But the recordings show the fish swimming back and forth in tight circles, as if they were displaying."

Whatever the fish were doing as they drummed away, James had plenty of information to give to the city council, and they asked him to come and talk to them. He played them recordings of fish sounds, and explained how it was possible for a fish to make a noise that could be heard through the walls of a house. The councillors believed his explanation – "Enough to hire a cocky graduate student instead of the expensive engineers!" he told me with a smile. But the homeowners were different. They appreciated James's help, but were harder to convince. "Some said that there was no way a fish could produce a sound that could be heard inside a house."

Cape Coral residents might have learnt from others who had also experienced mystery noises from the ocean. In the 1970s, the US navy found that the sea was so full of strange sounds that they had to employ scientists to help them tell fish sounds from those made by enemy submarines. The scientists discovered that there were 120 different kinds of fish making the sea noisy. We now know that, around the world, there are ten times that number of types of fish that use sound to signal to each other. Even goldfish make noises!

In the 1980s, another bunch of householders were tormented by sea sounds. People living in houseboats on the Sausalito waterfront in California offered all sorts of explanations for the loud buzzings that were disturbing their sleep – everything from sewage outlets to faulty fridges. Here, too, it took a marine biologist to set them straight: Dr John McCosker.

"I know what that noise is," Dr McCosker told them. "It's the romantic hoo-hooing of the male toadfish during the mating season." It was,

he admitted, a pretty awful sound. "It's like that scene in every crummy war movie you ever saw, where all the B-29s are flying together in formation."

It took some work to convince the sleep-deprived residents of Sausalito that a fish about the size of a frankfurter was causing all the ruckus. Dr McCosker had to catch four toadfish and get them singing in a tank before people believed him. Then they took the toadfish to their hearts and put on the Sausalito Humming Toad-fish Festival, with music, feasting and people dressing up as toadfish. All this is no more than this little fish deserves, as it is a record-breaker; it makes its sounds by vibrating its swim bladder faster than hummingbirds can beat their wings – thousands of times a minute.

Just a year or so before James Locascio walked into the offices of Cape Coral city council, the Swedish navy had become alarmed by a sound they'd heard in their coastal waters. Was it, they wondered anxiously, some new kind of submarine? Their fears were laid to rest when a team of Swedish biologists told them that the sinister sound was made by herrings! The scientists had discovered that herring were producing high-pitched noises by swallowing air from the surface and then squirting it out through their bottoms. The same discovery was made at the same time by a team of Scottish researchers. Dr Ben Wilson was one of them.

"We noticed that individual fish released more bubbles when there were more fish in the tank with them. In other words, it seems that herring like to fart in company!" he says. The fish aren't just behaving like naughty schoolboys – they make the sounds to signal to each other and to keep the shoal together. For small fish like herring, there is safety in numbers.

But no one in Cape Coral knew about any of that. So James set out to prove that he was right about the drum fish. He asked people experiencing the worst disturbance from the "mystery" noises to write down exactly when they heard them and how bad they were. The residents' records matched the timing of the fish-noises perfectly.

"I invited some of them to the dock to listen, so they could hear the sound live," James told me. He also explained why the noise was so loud in the houses, when you couldn't hear it at all standing by the water. "The water surface is a perfect reflector of sound, so sound does not escape through it. Fishes can be right near you but you can't hear the sound they make below the surface." At last, everyone was convinced!

There was no solution to the problem in

Cape Coral, but once people knew the noise was just their fishy neighbours they felt better. "And," James recalls, "the sound did go away at the end of the mating season in March." Of course, that also meant that it came back at the start of the mating season in November. And it comes back every year, from November to March. James doesn't study drum fish any more, but he still gets the occasional call from one of the Cape Coral residents, kept awake by that constant thumping buzz.

The more we listen to the sounds of the sea, the more we learn about the noises fish make. Fish have been recorded chorusing for hundreds of kilometres along the Pacific coast of America, their sound spreading like a Mexican wave in a football crowd. Even baby fish have been found to make a racket: young grey snappers make knocking and bumping sounds at night to keep in touch. There are mysteries, too. Sinking hydro-phones into deep waters more than 600 metres down off America's East Coast has allowed sci-entists Rodney Rountree and Francis Juanes to record twelve sounds that have never been heard before. They probably come from fish, but which fish and why they make the sounds has still to be discovered. We're just beginning to find out about how important sounds are to the lives of animals in the sea. And fish sounds are certainly important to animals that aren't fish – the ten fish that dolphins catch most often are those that make noises!

Shhhh!

Not every mystery sea sound is a fish, however. In 2013, people living in the seaside town of Hythe on the south coast of England began complaining about what teacher Val Cacchi called a "pulsing, droning noise, like an aeroplane that never goes away". It began at night when everything else was quiet, and just like Cape Coral, no one could work out where the sound was coming from. But no one went down to the waterside and listened to what was happening with a hydrophone. Instead, a reporter rang Ben Wilson, the herring-sound man, at his research lab in Scotland. There was, Ben said, a fish called the "midshipman" that made a noise like that, but it lived in the North Pacific, a very long way indeed from Hythe.

Sometimes facts are not allowed to get in the way of a good news story. Pretty soon newspapers, and TV and radio stations were reporting

that the little midshipman fish was making life in Hythe a misery.

"As far as I know," Ben Wilson told me, "there isn't a shred of evidence that the mystery noise in Hythe was created by a fish, or anything living. Perhaps it was a freezer in somebody's kitchen!" It seems pretty unfair that a little fish, minding its business half a world away, got blamed for noisy nights in an English seaside town. Still – that humans for you!

Monkey Business

O N the morning of 21 October 2007, Mr S.S. Bajwa, the Deputy Mayor of Delhi, India's capital city, was rushed to hospital with head injuries so severe that he sadly died. The next day newspapers carried the shocking headline "Deputy Mayor Killed By Monkeys". Now, the real story wasn't as strange as that makes it sound: poor Mr Bajwa wasn't murdered by a hit squad of monkey ninjas. What really happened was an accident. Some monkeys had come after food laid out on the balcony of the mayor's home. Mr Bajwa tried to fight them off, lost his balance and fell over the edge of the first floor balcony.

Even that sounds pretty strange. Whatever was a gang of monkeys doing in the middle of a city? And why were they bold enough to try

to steal the mayor's breakfast? To people who live in India, it isn't strange at all; gangs of monkeys are something they see almost every day. Two species of monkeys, the rhesus macaque and the bonnet macaque, a close relative, have made living alongside humans their speciality. Unlike other kinds of Indian monkey, which can only survive in wild forests that provide them with the right sort of food, rhesus and bonnet macaques can live anywhere and eat anything.

So they are able to make the most of the opportunities humans offer them, using buildings for shelter, electricity cables as above ground roads and eating human food. Now, in villages, towns and cities, at railways stations, the side of roads or canals, wherever there are humans, there are macaques, too.

Macaques get their hands on human food in whatever way they can. That might mean raiding an orchard for ripe fruit, or turning over a dustbin to find scraps; it could mean snatching vegetables from a market stall or climbing through an open window to steal food. Many Indian homes have wire grilles on their windows, but young monkeys are small enough, and hungry enough, to get through the smallest holes.

Once inside they open cupboards and fridges, and take whatever they can. What they can't eat on the spot or carry off with them, they stuff in their cheek pouches – sacs of skin at the sides of their faces. Macaques are good at running on three limbs!

They don't stop at shoplifting and burglary: they're also known for highway robbery. Anyone carrying something that looks like it might be edible is at risk. First, a monkey will approach and look you in the eye with an open mouth and bared teeth. This may look like a smile, but in macaque language it isn't a greeting, it's a threat; the macaque way of saying, "Give me your food now or I'll do something worse." If it doesn't work, the macaque will take the threat to the next level: a low grunt, then a slap or a sudden lunge, then a grab at your legs to throw you off balance. Finally, if you still won't let go of your sandwiches, it will bite.

Macaques are often described as working in gangs; a market stallholder will say that one monkey distracted her while its friends stole her tomatoes. But they don't really work together in this way. They are no good at sharing and fight over the tastiest morsels; it's just that when there is a possibility of a meal, several monkeys may get interested. So, there will be more than one trying to scare you into handing over your lunch, which can seem like a "gang attack". (This could be what happened to poor Mr Bajwa.)

Strangely, the fact that macaques aren't good at sharing is one of the things that makes them so good at adapting to life alongside humans. Macaques like living together but they have a very strict ranking system. The top monkeys get the best of everything – the food that is easiest to get and the tastiest to eat. Everybody else has to scrabble around fighting over what's left behind. And that's why these macaques investigate everything, just in case it turns out to be good to eat. So they spot any new opportunity and learn how to make the most of it – fast! They once even worked out how to open the motion-sensitive doors into the All India Institute of Medical Science, and ran about inside snatching patients' meals and testing medical equipment for food potential!

This habit of investigating any place or any object that might lead to food makes macaques even more of a nuisance to humans. They carry off all sorts of things, just in case they *do* turn out to be edible. Mobile phones, reading glasses, cameras, wallets and tablets all disappear, taken by their clever little hands. In 2014, in Shimla in northern India, banknotes rained down into the street because a macaque had stolen what looked like a promising bundle from a house, only to find it was just inedible bits of paper – which the monkey threw away, one by one.

Macaques' "bite now in case it's edible" appoach has also proved very bad news for India's plans to connect everyone to high-speed broadband. The government has pledged to connect every city, town and village to the internet by 2020. In a country the size of India, where more than a billion people live, that takes a *lot* of cable – 700,000 kilometres

of it, in fact. In many places burying the cable is impossible, so instead it is strung, unprotected, above ground.

A representative of the company installing the cables, Dinesh Malkani of Cisco Systems, confidently told a reporter, "We've built outdoor Wi-Fi access routers specifically keeping in mind Indian environmental conditions." But macaques' teeth weren't among the environmental conditions they were prepared for. In the city of Varanasi, cable was laid along the sacred River Ganges, beside the many temples where thousands of macaques have made their homes. The monkeys decided that the cable needed a thorough chewing, just to make *certain* it wasn't something laid on for their dinner. But by the time they had found out that broadband cable wasn't very tasty, the damage was done – and Varanasi's plans for Wi-Fi on every street corner lay in chewed-up ruins.

Another crime macaques have been known to commit is kidnapping. Back in 1943, Uma Grover was playing in the courtyard of her family's home in Delhi when a macaque snatched her baby cousin and carried her up a tree! Luckily the monkey wasn't trying out human baby as lunch. Macaques sometimes steal each other's babies, perhaps because young monkeys who haven't had their own babies are curious. So Uma's cousin was probably snatched by a young female attracted by the crying of the baby, which sounds a bit like a young monkey. Uma's family were of course very upset and worried, but, as always, macaques are more interested in where the next meal is coming from than anything else.

"After an hour, the monkey got bored," Grover told a newspaper years later. "It climbed down from the tree and traded my cousin for a stack of chapatis."

Thankfully macaques haven't made a habit of baby snatching – this is the only known case – but there's no doubt that the monkey problem in India and Malaysia is getting worse. One reason is that there are simply more monkeys and more people sharing the same space. Brianne Beisner, from the California National Primate Research Centre, studies macaques and she told me that, since the 1990s, macaque numbers have been rising dramatically. I wondered if the monkeys were getting cheekier too. "Certainly!" Brianne said. "Rhesus macaques in particular are becoming bolder and more aggressive towards humans."

Brianne's colleagues are reporting that this boldness is spreading to other, usually "better behaved" monkeys, like lion-tailed macaques, which are beginning to raid tea plantations in southern India.

What can be done to put a stop to the monkey crime wave? Luckily for the macaques, shooting and poisoning are out of the question because, to followers of Hinduism, the main religion in India, monkeys are sacred as the special creatures of the monkey-god Hanuman. For thousands of years they were allowed to live in Hindu temples, where they were fed and protected. This means that for every person chasing a macaque off with a stick, someone round the corner will be feeding another! While the first lot of macaques tore around inside the Institute of Medical Science, a second lot was being fed by the relatives of sick patients, in the hope that Hanuman would make their loved ones well again. In some cities, the naughty monkeys even get a feast laid on for them once a week in honour of Hanuman, so they have plenty of energy to go back to their life of crime on the other six days! Tourists don't help matters either. They don't have to live with the monkeys day in, day out and think their bared-teeth threats are "cute smiles", which they reward by handing over food. So the monkeys learn that being aggressive to humans is the perfect way to get an easy meal. In places where tourists feed monkeys, they are much more likely to bite. But in spite of posters in popular tourist spots telling people not to feed monkeys, it still goes on.

In Delhi, the city council tried using another sort of monkey as a kind of animal-policeman. Grey langur monkeys are quite common in India, and are much bigger than rhesus and bonnet macaques. So it was thought that they could be used to chase off their pesky smaller cousins. Captive grey langurs were taken around the city on leads, to chase troupes of macaques out of posh gardens and swanky terraces. But langurs are quite laid-back and gentle (when they live close to humans they tend to beg quietly for food rather than steal it). They can chase macaques off for a few minutes, but the cheeky monkeys come straight back or just go to the next house. All the same, when keeping captive langurs was banned there was an illegal trade in langur police-monkeys. Some people also began to make a living as monkey impersonators, copying the langurs' barking calls, and even dressing in monkey suits! These impersonators were employed to try and chase macaques out of the buildings and streets around the Indian parliament, where the little criminals were terrorising MPs and officials. None of this worked very well.

Stopping macaques from having so many babies would reduce the problem over time. But to prevent females from getting pregnant, they need to be given a pill every day – and this is very difficult to do when macaques fight over every bit of food. The top-ranking female is likely to eat all the treats with pills hidden inside, leaving the others without a single one! In one part of India, female macaques were caught and given an operation so they couldn't have more babies. But this costs a lot of money – and anyway, the monkeys soon learnt to avoid getting caught.

The effect that macaques have on people in India is huge. But it's hard to tell exactly how huge. You can count the fields of crops destroyed, the kilometres of cables chewed up, but it's harder to count up the hours people spend chasing monkeys off their land, or trying to keep them out of their houses.

"There are often hidden problems," Brianne says, "like the possibility that macaques may carry diseases that humans could catch." This is because macaques are so closely related to humans, and it could be a big problem for us in future. It was certainly a problem for macaques in the past. Because humans and macaques are so similar, newly discovered medicines were tested on them. Throughout the 1960s and 70s, Indian rhesus macaques were caught and sold to medical research projects around the world. Tens of thousands of monkeys lived out their days in laboratory cages, so that doctors could find ways to cure human diseases like small-pox, polio and rabies. They were used in space research, too, and even sent into orbit, which must have been a terrifying experience for a poor little monkey. The female macaque Miss Sam, who went up in a rocket in 1960, looks to me very unhappy indeed in all the photographs that were taken before the launch. Perhaps she knew that, for her, it would be a one-way trip.

Brianne and her team are about to start a big new research project to try and find a solution to the problems with macaques in India and other parts of Asia. But I can't help feeling that all the difficulties macaques are now causing could be just a bit of what Hindus call "karma" – the idea that if you do something bad, it'll come back to get you! In the Hindu epic, the Ramayana, the god Hanuman leads an army of monkeys to rescue the goddess Sita from the demon Ravana. Perhaps Hanuman is raising a new army – an army of mischievous marauding macaques, getting their own back on human beings for all those monkey lives spent behind bars.

The Bad Boys of Alaska

I'VE spent weeks and weeks of my life far out at sea in small boats, watching sperm whales. Of all the animals I have seen in the wild, they are for me the weirdest, which is probably part of the reason I like them so much. For a start, they are a peculiar shape: not graceful and streamlined like blue whales or humpbacks, but more like a blunt torpedo with a huge square head. A sperm whale's head takes up a third of its body length. If your head was in the same proportion, your chin would be where the middle of your chest is. Their blowhole – the whale's nostril through which they breathe – is in an odd place too. Other whales have their blowholes on the top of their heads (baleen whales like blues and humpbacks have two; toothed whales like sperm whales, orcas and dolphins have one).

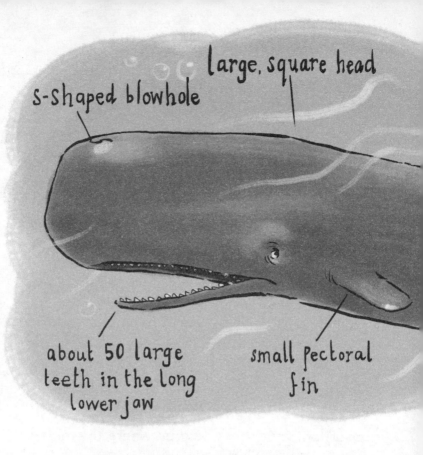

large, square head

s-shaped blowhole

about 50 large
teeth in the long
lower jaw

small pectoral
fin

A sperm whale's blowhole is in the top lefthand corner of its square snout, so when it surfaces and breathes out, the puff of breath, or "blow", is on a slant.

This is useful for a human observer, because you see that slanting blow and square head and

small hump instead
of a dorsal fin

long ridges
down the back

large tail
(flukes)

you immediately know that you are looking at a
sperm whale. In the warm tropical oceans where
I have watched sperm whales, seeing one blow
usually means that you'll see more. These waters
are where the females live, in family groups of
mums, sisters, nieces, grannies and their calves.

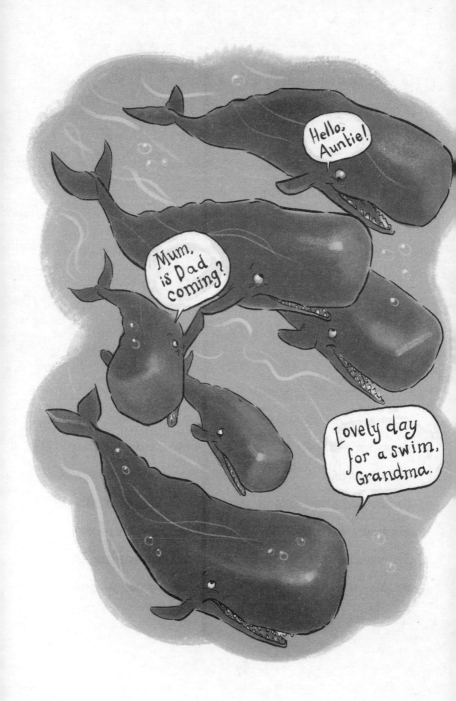

So there's a pretty good chance that once you've spotted a single blow, you'll soon see a group of sperm whales lolling about at the surface, chatting away to each other, making the loud clicking sounds they use to communicate.

If you're really lucky, you may see this extended family on the day that Dad comes visiting. Males wander the oceans, finding food in deep water as far north and south as the poles, and visiting different groups of females. Of course, all sperm whales are big: even a newborn calf weighs a tonne and is about as long as a family car (four metres). Females grow to roughly the length of a bus – around twelve metres – but males get really huge at eighteen metres, and twice the weight of the females. It's very exciting to see one, and when one of these big boys comes calling, it's sperm whale party time!

But sperm whales have another life under

the ocean, a thousand or more metres deep. Down there, they aren't relaxed "party animals" but efficient predators, using their clicks for another purpose – echolocation. That huge head is full of oil, which works as a lens for sound. Just as a lens in a pair of spectacles bends and focuses light, so the oil-filled head of the sperm whale shapes sounds. The whales' clicks are focused into a beam of sound. Echoes of these clicks bounce back and the sperm whale's big brain processes them to make a more detailed picture in sound (like the ultrasound that doctors use to see inside our bodies). So a sperm whale can locate and catch fast-moving prey like squid and fish in the deep, deep ocean, where there is no light at all. When you are floating in a boat over a group of sperm whales hunting in the deep water beneath you, their clicks sound like some kind of mad clock-factory. Every so often you'll hear a creaking sound. This is when the clicks get so close together that they run into each other – it means a whale has got very close to its prey and has probably managed to catch it.

No one has ever seen exactly what sperm whales get up to down there, but once, in the Sea of Cortez, I got a glimpse of a sperm whale's predator side. We were observing a large, very relaxed group of about thirty females and calves, resting at the surface in calm, clear waters. Just behind our boat, a metre-long Humboldt squid – a favourite sperm whale dinner – suddenly appeared. I don't know what made this creature decide on a trip to the surface from the deep waters it normally inhabits, but it soon found out that it was a bad idea.

A female sperm whale on the edge of the group spotted the squid at once and turned towards it, fast. Very, very, very fast. Realizing its fatal mistake, the squid dived, and the sperm whale follow-ed. I'll never forget the sight of that bright scarlet squid against the blue of the deep water – pursued by the sperm whale, like a grey guided missile. She moved with such precision and pur-pose, you could almost hear her brain working out just how quickly that squid was going to be toast. In less than a heartbeat, they had both disappeared into the dark depths.

I was left breathless. It was like finding out that your granny is really a cat burglar, or a Formula One racing driver. I found myself wondering how it would feel to have all that speed, power and intelligence turned against you. This is what some of the fishermen of Sitka in southern Alaska are finding out.

Less than 30 kilometres off the coast of southern Alaska, the seabed drops away to depths of a thousand metres and more. "Drop-offs" like this are exactly the kind of place that sperm whales like to do their hunting. But the waters are too cold for females and their calves, so it's the big males who come here to feed.

It's a good place for human fishermen, too; they come to catch the sable fish or black cod. These fish don't look like much – dark grey and ugly – but they are delicious and they fetch a high price. However, they aren't easy fish to land. They live 400 to 1,000 metres below the surface. To get a decent catch, each boat must set out four to ten kilometres of lines carrying thousands of baited hooks, all sunk to the right depth. It can take several hours to set out these "longlines", and several more to haul them back. Crews often work all night to bring in the lines and take the fish off the hooks, and then start again at dawn, baiting hooks and setting out more lines. It is hard, dangerous work even in good weather – but when the sea is rough and the wind is blowing? Well, you have to be seriously tough.

Sperm whales love black cod, too, and during the 1970s and 80s a whale would take fish from a longline once in a while, but it wasn't a big problem. Humans were only allowed to go after black cod for five days in every year, to make sure they didn't take too many. This wasn't enough time for sperm whales to learn about how humans were hauling their favourite prey up from the deep. But in 1995 that all changed. A limit was set on how many black cod each fishing boat could take in a year, but they could fish for them on as many days as they liked. So, instead of all the boats going after black cod on the same five days, boats were longlining for them from March to November, whenever there was good weather.

The sperm whales had a lot of time and opportunity to figure out that they didn't have to chase fish to get their dinner; all they had to do was hang around a fishing boat until the lines were hauled in, and steal the fish off the hooks. They didn't touch the red rockfish that the longlines also caught – just their favourite, black cod.

Within three years, it was common for fisher-men to lose part of their catch to thieving sperm whales as more of them learnt to plunder longlines. Now, a single boat can be surrounded by as many as ten male sperm whales. They hear the sound that the engine makes when the lines are set out and hauled in, and swim towards it from up to 50 kilometres away.

"It's like their dinner bell!" said one of the fishermen.

A boat can lose a thousand dollars' worth of fish as the hooks come up bent and empty after the sperm whales have taken their dinner.

Stephen Rhoads, the captain of a boat from the port of Sitka, says, "The whales are getting better at this every single year. It's less work for them to hang out with us and take our fish than it is to dive down and get them off the bottom." Scientists agree: they think that this way sperm whales can get four to seven times more food than they would by hunting naturally.

It may be easier for whales to take the cod off the lines than catch their own, but it still takes skill. The "dinner bell" sound from the fishing boats may travel for kilometres through the water, but the whales must learn to pick out that sound from all the others in the sea, and then home in on it.

Then there's the problem of getting a 50-centimetre fish off a five-centimetre hook attached to a line being hauled in, fast. Not easy for a male sperm whale 18-metres long. Scientists weren't sure how the whales were doing it, until they attached a video camera to a longline and caught a whale in the act. It used its long, thin lower jaw to hook the line and pull it tight, jerking the fish off the hook and into its mouth.

Successful thieving from longlines requires a quite remarkable set of new skills, and yet this ability has spread among the Sitka sperm whales very quickly. If every whale had to learn for itself then the fishermen of Sitka wouldn't have much of a problem, because that would take the whales a long time. One of the secrets of their ability to survive is that sperm whales can learn from each other. This means that new ways of doing things – like stealing black cod off longlines – can spread through groups and populations of animals very quickly.

Stealing fish from nets and fishing lines isn't just a sperm whale thing. Other species do it as well, and the ones who do it best and give humans the most trouble are the two next most sociable species, bottlenose dolphins and killer whales. Animals who learn from each other can quickly share new ways to survive, just as humans share things like how to read or drive a car or the latest craze in clothes or boy bands.

We know how we share and learn from each other, but we are not yet sure exactly how sperm whales do it. Does one whale learn by simply watching another whale? Does one whale teach another? Or do they tell each other what to do? I asked my old friend Professor Hal Whitehead, who has studied sperm whales for 30 years.

"I suspect they listen a lot to each other," he told me, "and if they hear each other feeding, especially in new circumstances, they go over and investigate." So they learn pretty much the way you'd learn about a new game in the playground. Sperm whales certainly use their complicated clicking sounds to communicate; maybe one day we'll know just what they're saying. Perhaps in Alaska it'll be a long set of instructions about popping fish off longline hooks.

One thing we do know about the Sitka sperm whales is that they are all males, and usually hunt alone. This makes the fact that they have learnt from each other, and gather in large numbers around boats, more remarkable, because the males aren't known to hang out together much. Scientists have also discovered that although more than a hundred sperm whale males steal black cod, there are just ten individuals, nicknamed the "Bad Boys", who do it over and over again. One of these has been involved in so many fish heists on Sitka boats that the fishermen have nicknamed him "Jack the Stripper" because he's so good at stripping fish from their hooks!

Why are the Bad Boys such fish-stealing experts, and are they leading other whales into a life of fish-stealing crime? A team of scientists and fishermen who have formed the Southeast Alaska Sperm Whale Avoidance Project – SEASWAP for short – are trying to find answers, which could be the key to solving the problem of thieving sperm whales. So far, they have managed to put satellite tags on four of the ten Bad Boys. The hope is that they may be able to warn fishing boats about their location so the fishermen can avoid setting longlines nearby. But how successful this will be, we just don't know. As Captain Stephen Rhoads says, "One thing we do know is that these whales are very, very smart."

There was a time, more than 100 years ago, when sperm whales were hunted all over the world – including the waters off Alaska. The lamps of Europe and America burned using oil from the heads of hundreds of thousands of sperm whales. Jane Atkins, a TV producer who filmed Sitka's Bad Boys in action, put it very well when she said, "The tables have turned: whaling is banned, and sperm whales are returning and learning to take on fishermen in bold and surprising ways. And there's not a thing the fishermen can do about it."

Teaming Up

WE have a lot of words for animals that do things we don't like: "pest", "parasite", "vermin" ... even, as you've read in this book, "demon" and "devil". I'm sure if animals could use words, they'd have a few pretty nasty ones for us as well. But then, if animals *could* use words, we'd be able to speak to each other – imagine what a difference that would make! We would be able to explain to the macaques in Varanasi that broadband cables are never going to be a good meal; wolverines could tell us why they walk straight up the side of mountains; and perhaps we'd work out a deal with sperm whales, so they didn't take all the cod off the Alaskan fishermen's hooks!

Amazingly, even without using words, some humans and animals do manage to work together so that both get something that they want.

Honey is a precious food, especially to the bees who make it. On the grasslands of East Africa, wild bees build their hives deep inside hollow trees so they are hard to find. They guard their stores of honey by attacking and stinging any animal that comes looking. One sting is very painful; a couple of hundred could kill you. So if you want to eat honey, beeswax or the fat juicy baby bees – grubs that look like little white sausages – you have two problems: one, finding the hive, and two, avoiding a bad stinging. A little brown bird called a honey guide, related to our cuckoo, has the solution to problem one; humans have the solution to problem two. Honey guides can fly to places that humans can't see from the ground. They have sharp eyes and can smell honey from a distance. Humans have fire, and smoke makes bees sleepy and much less likely to sting. As humans and honey guides have lived together in East Africa for hundreds of thousands of years, they have found a way to talk to each other so they can put their two solutions together.

It begins with a piercing whistle and tapping on a hollow tree. This is the human saying to the honey guide, "Hey! You ready?" The little bird replies with a call that sounds like a rusty hinge squeaking over and over. This is the honey guide's way of saying, "OK. I'm ready!" It only ever uses this call when it's talking to humans.

So the humans whistle and the bird creaks back. Each time it creaks it moves a little further, and the humans follow. On and on they go, through the grass and trees and bushes, until they get to the right tree. There, the honey guide makes a different call and flies around so the humans understand that it's saying, "*This* is the place."

Then it's time for the humans to provide the solution to problem number two. They light a fire and tie together some smouldering leaves or sticks. They climb into the tree with the smoking bundle and poke it into the hole where the bees have their hive. While the bees are dozy from the smoke, the humans pull out the waxy comb stuffed with honey and bee grubs. They keep the honey and leave a big chunk of comb with bee grubs in it for the honey guide, so both bird and humans get a feast.

In Brazil, there's another two-part problem that animals and humans solve together. The southern Brazilian city of Laguna stands on a river where it meets the sea. Every autumn, big schools of mullet swim up the river from the ocean. They are hard to catch; the water is murky, so it's difficult to spot the fish, and the river is wide, so there's plenty of room for them to escape. Like sperm whales, bottlenose dolphins also use sound to find their food. They click and whistle, then listen to the echoes of their voices to give them a "sound picture" of what's around them. So they have the solution to part one of the mullet-catching problem – finding fish in muddy water. Humans, with circular fishing nets that they throw over the water, have the solution to part two.

In mullet-migration season, fishermen go down to the river and wade into the shallow water. They splash the surface with their nets or hands to let the dolphins know that they are ready to begin. The dolphins signal back with a tail slap or two. The fishermen know each dolphin from the shape of its tail and dorsal fin, and have names for them, like "Escubi" or "Filipe". Their favourite dolphins are the ones who are the best at signalling to them where and when to throw their nets. They call them *botos bon* ("good dolphins") and they call out to them by name. A dolphin will leap out of the water, its nose pointing in the direction that the fish are swimming. The height of the leap tells the fishermen how big a school of fish the dolphin has spotted using echolocation. The dolphin will then slap its tail or roll to tell the fisherman, "Throw your net *now*!" The net whirls in the air

and lands in the water like a spider web. The fish have nowhere to escape to – they are trapped between the nets, the fishermen's legs, and the fast-swimming dolphin! The net comes in full and

the dolphin gets a big fish that might otherwise have escaped upriver.

It's hard to tell exactly how or when humans, honey guides and dolphins first began to work together like this. But one thing is for sure: these relationships began with humans and animals really looking at and listening to each other. Most modern humans pay very little attention to nature, and nowadays cooperation between humans and animals is very rare. Perhaps if we paid more attention, we'd find out what life could be like if we cooperated with animals a bit more, and learnt some of the lessons they have to teach us.

Thanks

The real life stories and information in this book were gathered by scientists and film-makers who study and document animal behaviour in the wild. They tolerated my endless questions and shared their knowledge with great generosity. There isn't space to mention everyone here, but at least I can thank Mark Scafford, John Aitchison, Justine Evans, Judy Diamond, Alan Bond, James Locascio, Ben Wilson, Brianne Beisner, Hal Whitehead, Claire Spottiswoode and Nathan Emery.